The Hidden iPad Guide: Tips, Tricks, and Techniques for Complete Mastery of your iPad Even If You're A Complete Beginner

Table of Contents

Summary

You probably are thinking about getting yourself a new iPad or any other electronic tablet or you already have one. Perhaps you own one or more for your personal use of for the library and you are wondering if you are really getting the most out of your device. This book is basically a sharing and demonstration session so you better pull out your iPad as and do the practical things as you read along. This book will especially address itself on the subject of Apps and other ideas that will help use some hidden functions most iPad owners know nothing about. Get to learn how to best watch your TV and movies, listen to audio books and music as well as the easiest way to stay in touch using Twitter, Facebook and other social media websites.

Introduction

The iPad you just bought or are thinking of buying is such a wonderful device and there is no wonder it has captivated the attention of millions of people globally. From the time the first iPad was released by Apple sometime in 2010, there has been exaltation among the population because of its splendid touch screen functions and high speed web browsing facilities.

Today there is even the iPad mini that is so functional the teens and kids find it easy to use. The sleek nature of these devices from Apple Inc That come loaded with videos and games is made even better due to the clarity that is yet to be superseded by any other brand. Think about the photos that are taken by the iPad that are so real people looking at them almost feel close to the moment when the picture was taken.

With the weight of the iPad being less than a kilogram, carrying it everywhere you go has become a must for owners. This device can easily fit in your handbag and you feel comfortable carrying it around. You can use it conveniently sitting on the bed or lying on your couch and you can be sure you will not need your laptop for a while now. What with a battery life that exceeds that of the laptop ender normal circumstances; you and your kids can read books and play games uninterrupted. Take time to learn a few secrets so you can get the best out of your device.

Buying your iPad

Currently there are five different types of iPads available in two different sizes; you can choose between Wi-Fi and Mobile data with three different storage choices. What this means is that there are a whole sixty different iPad configurations. While the number may sound intimidating, you have no reason to worry because narrowing your choice to the right one for you is not a herculean task. The key to knowing what iPad to buy is having an understanding on what you will be using your iPad for.

The iPad Air 2 vs iPad Air vs iPad Mini 3 vs iPad Mini 2 vs iPad Mini

The newest kids on the block are the iPad Air 2 and the iPad Mini 3. Prices begin at $499 for the iPad Air 2 which is a good upgrade whose processing speed is enhanced at 40% with a 250% increase in graphics when compared to the iPad Air. This device has a highly improved camera as well as a Touch ID: you can use your thumbprint to sign into your iPad. With touch ID you can easily use the Apple Payment System without any hassles as long as you are online.

The price of the iPad 3 begins at $399; this does not have an upgraded processor when compared to its predecessor, the mini 3. Instead, it only has a Touch ID as the new feature. This gadget is similar to the mini 3 in many regards especially the graphics and processor speed.

Initializing your iPad

After buying your iPad and pulling it out of the box, what do you do next? You must begin the process of setting it up so you can use it for the first time. The good news is that the process is not at all complicated and you can do it without having the device connected to your PC. All that you need to know is your Wi-Fi password if your area has a secured network. With this information at hand you only need about 5 minutes and your iPad will be up and running.

Steps for initializing an iPad:

Start the Process: The first step you must take to get your iPad up and running is to swipe across the bottom of the screen from left to right. This communicates to the iPad that you want to start using it; you will repeat the same action every other time you would like to use the device.

Language setup: Tell the iPad the language you love to communicate with. English is the default setting but several other languages that are supported.

Choice of country or region: Your iPad will ask what country you are located in so it can connect you with the appropriate version of the Apple App Store. This is because some Apps are unavailable in other countries.

Select a Wi-Fi Network: If you live in network secured area, this is where you will need the Wi-Fi password.

Enable Location Services: Location services are used to allow your device to determine where the iPad is located. Even the older versions that don't have 4G or GPS make use of location services by using Wi-Fi services in determining location. Most people start with this particular App for starters; but it can be turned off later when you have downloaded other similar Apps.

Set up as New or Restore from Backup: As soon as you purchase your iPad, you set it up as new. However, if you encounter problems later that will require you fully restore your iPad, you can choose between iTunes to restore the backup or Apple's iCloud service. When you are restoring from a backup, the gadget will ask you to input your iCloud username and password followed by which backup you want to restore. However, when it's your first time to activate your iPad, simply select "Set Up as New iPad".

Create new Apple ID: If you have been using another Apple device such as an iPhone or an iPod, or if you have used iTunes to download music, you don't have to create a new Apple ID because you already have one. Use the same Apple ID to sign in to your iPad. The good news about doing it this way is that your music can be re-downloaded without having to pay for it again. However, if it's your first time to use an Apple Device, you must create an Apple ID. If you have the ID already, enter the username, which is usually an email address followed by your password.

Accept Terms and Conditions: There are terms and conditions you need to agree to before the iPad can give you a dialog box confirming that you did. The same can be emailed to you if you desire at the touch of a button at the top of the screen.

Set Up iCloud: You most likely will want to setup the iCloud so your iPad can be backed up daily. The advantage of this is that even if your iPad malfunctioned or even gets stolen, all your data will be backed up and waiting for you to restore or replace the iPad. However, for those who are reluctant to save any data on the internet for any reason whatsoever, simply decline the offer to use iCloud.

Use Find My iPad: Don't ignore this feature; it is so crucial it will help you recover a lost or stolen iPad. When this feature is turned on it helps in tracking the general direction of your device. The 3G version comes with a GPS chip which makes it even more accurate. However, even the Wi-Fi version is also very accurate.

iMessage and FaceTime: With this feature anyone can contact you using the email address you used as your Apple ID. You can take FaceTime calls – this is video conferencing software akin to iMessage texts or Skype. This allows you send and receive messages to family and friends using your iPad, iPhone or iPod Touch. Those who already have iPhones will see their phone numbers listed alongside their email addresses associated with their Apple ID.

Siri: If you have an iPad that supports Siri, it will prompt you on whether you want to use it or not. Siri is Apple's voice recognition system that you can use to perform several tasks which include searching for a pizza café or setting up a reminder etc.

Diagnostics: Finally, you have to choose whether or not the iPad will send daily diagnostic reports to Apple. If you choose to use this feature which is really optional, Apple uses the information it receives to improve its services to you and other customers. You don't have to worry about how the information will be used but if you have any fears, choose not to share the information.

Get Started: Now that you have initialized your iPad, the final thing you should do is to click on the "Get Started" icon that is found on the "Welcome to iPad" page.

With these simple steps you will have finalized the setting up of your iPad.

iPad 101: The basics of using the iPad for Newbie's

If you are new to the iPad, you don't have to worry because the following simple lessons will give you a flying start. Taking these lessons allows you to get the most and best out of your iPad's experience. This guide will try to cover as mush as possible of what a new iPad user needs to know.

Usually, after you have bought a new iPad and have already taken the initializing steps you will be ready to start using it. What follows does not have to stress you. You can only consider yourself a greenhorn if you have never used an iPhone or an iPod Touch. This is because many applications such as locating and installing good Apps, organizing or even deleting them, navigating the iPad

iPad Navigation and Using the iPad Home Button

A great deal of navigation on your iPad will be done using simple touch gestures: you only need to touch an icon to launch an

application or swipe your finger to the left or right across your screen if you are trying to move from one icon to another. Depending on the application you are using, you can use the same gesture to do different things: these icons actually have some common sense.

A good example is when you are swiping a finger across your screen that will move you from one screen filled with application icons when you are at the home screen; you use the same gesture to move from one book page to another when using the iBooks application. Apart from tapping your screen and moving a finger across the screen, you may also have to touch the screen and hold a finger down. When holding your finger down against an app icon and you keep it there, the mode you enter allows you to move that icon to a different location on the screen.

The iPad Home Button

Apple has designed the iPad such that there are very few buttons on its exterior with the Home Button being on of them. The button is the circular button that sits square at the bottom of the iPad. This is the button you use to wake up the iPad from sleep and is also used to exit applications. You may want to consider the Home Button as the "Go Home" button that is used at any moment whether the iPad was idling or you were inside an application.

Welcome to the world of iPad Apps

There are well over 300,000 Apps that have been designed to be compatible with your iPad with many more being compatible with iPhone Apps. This makes it quite difficult for anyone trying to locate what can be termed as a good App. The good news is there are simple ways you can locate a good App.

Instead of trying to search the iPad App Store directly, one of the simplest ways is to search through Google. You only need to use the "type of App" you are looking for as the keyword and you will be home and dry. Instead of searching for Apps page by page through the store, simply go to Google and type "the best iPad … followed by the type of App. Search the Apps store after you have already targeted the particular App you discovered.

While Google gives you a short cut in locating the desired Apps, this will not always give you the best results. This is the reason we give you a few other tips that allow you to find great Apps without so much of a hassle:

Featured Apps

This is the first tab you will find at the very bottom of the App Store; since Apple has selected these particular Apps as the best among their different categories, you should have no doubt about their quality. Apart from the featured Apps, you will also be able to notice new as well as other noteworthy Apps that are listed by Apple Staff members as among favorites.

Top Charts

This Tab lists Apps in terms of popularity. Even though popularity is not necessarily a good way of ascertaining the quality of a product, you will not always go wrong if you looked here. The Top Charts Tab is normally divided into different categories that users can choose from. Once you choose your preferred category, you can go beyond the most popular Apps by swiping from the top to the bottom of the list using your finger. Always use this gesture on your iPad when you scroll down any lists or when going down a particular page on a website.

Sort by Customer Rating

The other way you can search for a good App is using the search window that is found in the screen's top right hand corner. The results will be delivered beginning with the "most relevant" as a way of assisting you to locate a specific App even though the quality may not be always guaranteed. The better way to do this type of search is choosing to sort your search results using ratings given by users. This is done by tapping on "By Relevance" followed with "By Rating". Don't forget to look at "By Rating" so you can see the number of times it has been rated. You can be sure that if you get a 4-Star App that has been rated more than 200 times, it is likely to be better than a 5-star App that has been rated only 4 or 5 times.

Leading "must have" iPad Apps

You have learned a few things about your iPad and the whole world of Apps and are now ready to fill it up with Apps. Since there are so many, you may not be sure what to download especially when you are just beginning. Visiting an Apps Store that keeps tens of thousands of some of the best Apps available anywhere can be compared to looking for a needle in a haystack. In this guide we show you some of the leading Apps you can download without paying a dime. This is the reason we include them among "must have" iPad Apps that you should download from that iPad Apps Store.

Crackle

If you are a fan of movies, there is no doubt you adore Hulu Plus and Netflix, some of the leading movie Apps known to-date. Come in Crackle and you have an App that delivers great movies and TV shows that comes with an interface that goes beyond Hulu Plus and far beyond the experience you could have had with Netflix. But what's more, this App comes to you free of charge and without the burden of having to pay periodic subscriptions. This is what qualifies

Crackle to be among the best "must have" iPad Apps that delivers free TV Shows and movies.

iWork

iWork is an Apps suite that is loaded with several Office Apps that Apple used to give for free to anyone purchasing a new iPad after the iPhone 5S was released. The best part of the bargain is that it doesn't matter whether you are buying the latest generation of the iPad: all you need to do is buy a new iPad. The iWork suite comes with a word processor (Pages), spreadsheets (numbers) as well as presentation software (keynote). Even though these will not necessarily replace Microsoft Office, this is definitely an App that will enhance your business productivity in one way or another.

Google maps

Google Maps is such a great one such that Tim Cook had to apologize after Apple came up with its own version known as Maps App. There is no way you can compare the newer Maps App with the well known Google maps which has continued to improve. You can easily convert your iPad into a GPS or a map route before you begin your journey; you have Google maps to thank for that. This is an extremely functional iPad App that you should download for free from your App Store.

Evernote

Evernote operates like the popular Notes App that comes with your iPad but this one comes loaded with a number of highly-charged features. This App is cloud-based and, as such, you need to open an account which you sign into every time you want to retrieve your data. What this simply means is that you can sign in to your Evernote account using any Android device, your Pc or the iPad itself. The App allows you to create task lists and notes which you can email from your Evernote account and also use tags to organize them.

Pandora

If we have spoken about TV, Movies and games among our list of "must have" Apps, you may think we are living out music; nothing could be further from the truth. The Pandora App for iPads comes simple but very sleek and offers you the versatility of a music website minus the related clutter. This allows you to enjoy your music in the background even as you work. Combine this App with features like home sharing and the ability to gain access to your entire collection of music and you can begin imagining how the iPad is going to replace your valued home stereo. Pandora is perhaps one of the leading Apps available for your iPad and to think that you don't have to pay for it makes it even better.

Flipboard

If you are willing to completely transform your experience of social media into what can be called an interactive magazine, then Flipboard is what marries Twitter, Facebook, Flickr and several other social media websites with the renowned news magazine websites such as Sports Illustrated and CNN to create a tailor-made magazine that intertwines itself with your entire social experience. If you have already been wowed by Twitter or Facebook, then wait until you have an experience with Flipboard turning them into a magazine.

iBooks

iBooks provides you with the ultimate eBook reader of choice making it among the leading "must have" iPad Apps for your gadget. If you have a voracious appetite for books, you don't need to stop at iBooks. This is because your iPad supports others such as Barnes & Noble Nook, Kindle as well as the Stanza reader thus giving you a host of options to choose from just to satisfy your thirst for reading.

Yelp

Perhaps you love eating out and are bored with visiting the same old restaurants whose menu and everything else have become so common place to you; nothing comes close to Yelp in helping you to locate some of the best establishment around you that you probably know nothing about. This powerful App also features a host of reviews from other people who have been there before. Apart from locating restaurants within your vicinity, you can be sure to get information about the best among them. If your iPhone already has this App, there is no harm transitioning to the one on iPad which is definitely better.

Facebook

It's in open secret that Facebook controls a lion's share among social media sites that people use in keeping in touch with friends and family. The iPad has integrated Facebook into the bowels of its operating system and, as such, sharing websites and photos has never been this easier. Make sure you connect your iPad to your Facebook account before you download the App as this will enhance your experience. Coming

with the official Facebook account is a host of free clients for your Facebook and Twitter as well as several other social networks.

DropBox

If you are worried about storage and are looking for an extra 2GB of storage for your iPad free of charge, then DropBox is the answer to your problem. This is a cloud based storage solution that also makes it possible for you to share your files between all your devices. When you therefore you want to transfer photos from your iPad to your PC without struggling to look for a cable, you have it with DropBox. The same applies when you want to transfer your files from your PC to your iPad without a hassle.

How to install Apps

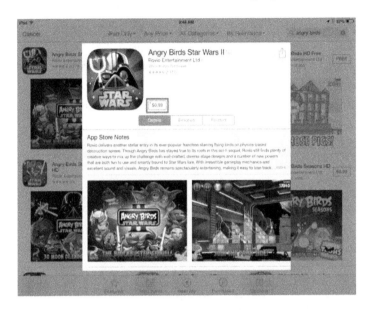

We have already shared with you a few Apps that are a "must have" but our list is in no way conclusive, there are many other great Apps you can avail so you can use your iPad to the maximum. Once you have located these great Apps and many others, the next logical step is to install them on your iPad.

The process of installing Apps is a simple two-step process. The first place for you to touch is the "Price" icon which is normally outlined in bold red. If you are interested in free Apps they will always read "FREE". As soon as you touch the button, its outline will turn green and read "INSTALL APP". As soon as you touch that button, the installation process starts automatically.

On the Apps page of the Apple Store, you will find the download button located on the top of the iPads screen above the details tab.

21

Apps can also be installed directly from your search results: simply touch the price tag you find on the right hand side of the search result box and consider it done.

After you have selected the App you want to install, there are chances you will be asked to enter your iTunes account password. This is a request that has been deliberately designed to protect your iPad in cases where anyone else picks your iPad and wants to download a couple of Apps without your authority. However, if you downloaded some Apps recently the iPad assumes you are still the one using it and will not therefore request a password. This lets the iPad not ask you for the password each time when you are downloading a couple of Apps all at once.

Moving Apps

After you have downloaded your favorite Apps from the Apps Store, the iPad could automatically place them on a second screen. Switching between screens is as simple as swiping a finger across the iPad. However, you may want to move a particular App so it can appear on the first screen where you have quick access to it.

This is a simple exercise: place your finger on the App's icon and hold it down firmly until the rest of the icons on that screen start jiggling; a few of them will show a black circle that has an "x" in the middle. This is called the "move state". With your iPad on the "move state", you should be able to move icons by holding a finger down on top of them as you slide your finger along. The targeted icon moves along with your finger as long as the finger stays on the screen.

If you are going to move a particular iPad App to a different screen, firmly hold your finger down on that icon for you to initiate the move and then move your finger up to the edge of the screen. Make sure to stop on the edge of the screen where its display shows the black edge at the iPads screen. This is because the iPad does not recognize your intention when you move you finger over or beyond that black edge.

When you move your finger towards the left hand side of the display, the iPad will shift the App to the screen on the left hand side. In the same manner, if you move the icon towards the right hand side it will be moved to the screen on the right hand side of the display. When the icon has reached the intended destination, place it by simply lifting your finger and you task is done.

Once you are done with moving any iPad Apps icons, the iPad will leave the "move state" when you click the Home Button. The Home Button is one among the few physical buttons you have on your iPad and like we said earlier, it is used to exit from anything else you are doing.

Deleting Apps

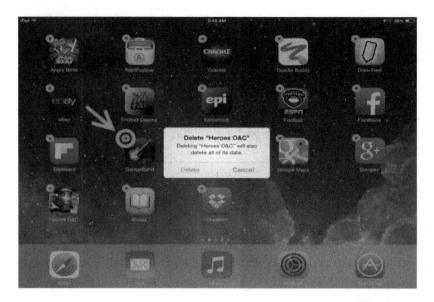

What do you do when you install and App on to your iPad only to discover later that it really does not satisfy you? Simple, follow this short procedure to delete it from your device; deleting an App follows a procedure that is similar to the one you used to move an App icon from one point to another.

Start by tapping and holding the particular icon until the rest of the icons on the screen start jiggling. This is the "move state" we mentioned earlier when discussing how to move Apps. We indicated when the iPad is in this state, a few icons have a black circle on top of them with the mark "x" in the middle.

To delete the icon, you only need to tap on the "x" button and the job is as good as done. In the event that you delete an App by mistake, you have no cause for alarm. The iPad always asks the user to confirm every choice they make about of deleting Apps before the action is executed.

Simply tap the "x" button to delete an App. don't worry about accidentally deleting an app. The iPad will confirm your choice before the app is actually deleted.

What if the App does not have an "x" button?

There are several Apps that are known as default Apps that normally come installed inside your iPad. These icons include Contacts, Calendar, Apps Store, iTunes, Games Center etc. which you are not allowed to delete. However, some of these applications can easily be removed by enabling the iPads parental controls.

Creating Folders and Organizing iPad Apps

You may also want to create a folder using the icons you have on your iPads screen. All you need to do is to enter the "move state"; touch an iPad App and hold a finger firmly on it until all the icons start jiggling.

Remember our tutorial on moving Apps? We learned that you can move any App around the screen as long as the finger is pressed down to the icon and move it on the display.

When you want to create a folder, all you need to do is to move one App and drop it directly on top of another App. Take note that when you move an App icon and place it on top of another one, the application will be highlighted with a square. This means therefore that you are able to create a folder the moment you lift the finger and in effect you drop the icon on top of it. You can also put a few other icons in the folder using the same simple procedure; drag them to the folder and simply drop them on it.

Once a folder has been created, you will be able to see a title bar bearing the name of the folder on it together with all its contents. You can rename the folder by simply touching the area with the title and once it is highlighted you can use the on-screen keyboard to type in the desired name. The iPad normally gives folders a smart name that is based on the functionality of the Apps you have decided to combine.

What do you do when you decide you want to access the icons in the folder? Simple, just tap on the folder and you have access to all its icons. Once you are in the folder and you want to exit, all you need to do is to tap on the iPad Home Button. Remember you use the Home Button to exit from any task you are doing on your iPad.

Using your iPad like a Pro

We have now covered all the basics and have gone on to download a bunch of iPad Apps but there is still one thing that is remaining. You need to personalize your iPad and make it your own unique gadget. There are many ways you can personalize your iPad and go beyond what most people do; many believe that personalization ends when you pick a uniquely colored Smart cover. This part of the guide will show you how you can place a customized picture on your iPad as a background, how to lock it using a passcode as well as customize several other iPad settings.

27

Use folders to organize your iPad

Many people don't know that they can customize their iPads including creating photos as well as personalized background images. Your iPad can accommodate many cool things that can help you make it truly personal; you don't have to remain with the generic interface settings that came with your iPad. We are going to explore a few unique ways you can use to customize your iPad experience.

One of the first things you are going to do with your iPad is to create folders for your icons, which is actually one of the basics. You should be able to dock your folders at the bottom of your screen so that you can always have easy access to the said applications. Even when you are unable to have quick access, you can easily use spotlight search – this is a search screen that is found on the left of your home screen – it helps you search for any movies, music or Apps. You should also be able to search the web using spotlight search. We have already learned how to create folders and, as such, we shall not repeat it here.

How to use spotlight search

Spotlight search is a powerful tool that helps you to easily access anything you have stored on your iPad. Whether you are looking for contacts, Apps, movies or music on your iPod touch, iPad or iPhone, the spotlight search helps you to avoid searching from one page to another for that App or having to go over your entire music collection.

To open the spotlight search, all you need to do is swipe down your iPad when you are not in any App. Avoid swiping from the very top of the screen else you will open the notification center. A screen bar appears at the top of the iPad when you have swiped down so that the on-screen keyboard pops up, start typing to begin your search.

Among the best features of the spotlight search is how quickly you are able to launch any App. When you have had an iPad for a while there a chances it is full of all types of Apps: these can be organized into folders but even then you can find yourself spending time looking for the particular App. This is where spotlight search comes in handy-you quickly run through the entire App population.

The same is true for people who have downloaded a large collection of music; you don't have to open the music App all the time and run through the entire list to look for some particular song or artist. All you need to do is a spotlight search and start typing the name of the song, band or artist. These actions quickly narrow your search results and, soon as you tap the song name; it is launched automatically on the music App. Even if you want search Wikipedia, you don't have to rush and open the Safari Browser, simply tap the "search Wikipedia" button found at the bottom of your results list and for Google just tap the : Search Web" button.

Add a Custom Keyboard

The latest gig that comes with your iPads Operating system is that it allows you to install some widgets on your iPad that include third-party keyboards: this can be used to replace the on-screen keyboard that comes by default. A widget is a miniature App that runs within other Apps and can easily be used to go beyond simply customizing the keyboard.

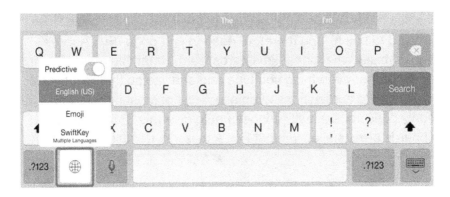

For you to install a custom keyboard you first have to download a keyboard from the Apps Store; the custom keyboard cannot be selected before you download it into your iPad. Go on and set it up as a "Third-Party Keyboard" in your device's setting and finally select the keyboard. There are a few popular alternative keyboards for iPads that include Swiftkey, Swype and PopKey which is yet to be released – this one resembles the Emoji keyboard only that it can use animated GIF images in the place of Smiley faces.

Setting up a Custom Keyboard on Your iPad

Go to your iPad's Settings App and on the left hand side menu select General to bring the general settings on the main window. Use your finger to scroll down the main window until you locate "Keyboard". When you tap "Keyboard" it will bring the settings for the on-screen keyboard.

At the top of the keyboard settings tap on "Keyboards" and then tap on "Add New Keyboard".

You will see a pop-up menu showing different keyboards and under "Suggested Keyboards" you will see "Third party keyboards". The keyboard App you downloaded earlier will be listed if it supports replacing the on-screen keyboard. All you need to do is to tap on the keyboard's name and it becomes your third party keyboard.

Once you have installed the keyboard, the iPad will still need to be instructed to use it. You therefore need to first go to "Full Access" because this is what some keyboards want. What this means is that they will gather everything you type and analyze so that in future it improves word suggestions even as you type. Most people who are security conscious usually choose not to give this "Full Access"; keyboards are installed without Full Access by default.

Use pictures to personalize your iPad

One of the easiest ways to personalize your iPad is to remove the default wallpaper background as well as the image the iPad uses on the lock screen. You may want to use the photos of you loved ones, friends or just about any image that you have found on the web; you want tour iPad to stand out and be different from any other one.

Since your iPad allows you set new and unique pictures as wallpaper both for its background and lock screen: this is the first screen that greets you first thing when you wake up.

Start by going to your iPads settings by tapping on the settings icon; it looks like a set of gears turning. Once there, select "Brightness & Wallpaper" on the left hand side of the menu on the settings screen.

When you choose Wallpaper in this screen you will be able to get a set of default themes that come to you from Apple by default or alternatively you can select Camera Roll so you can select from among the photos you have taken using your iPad. If your photo stream is turned on, you can easily choose one picture from the photo stream.

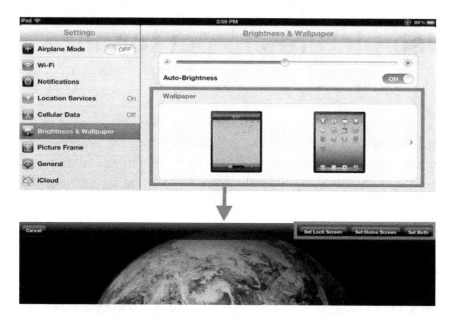

Once you have chosen a theme or a picture, the iPad will take you to a preview of the picture you have chosen to use as the background. Simply tap the button with the label "Set Lock Screen" to set the background or tap on "Set Home Screen" to set the photo as your lock screen. This photo or theme will automatically appear below your App icons; you can also choose "Set Both" so the picture can be used as your iPad's global background.

You can also use photos you have saved on your iPad from the web; you only need to hold a finger firmly down on any photo on the Safari Browser. If you love fun backgrounds, simply do a Google image search with the keyword "Image search for iPad backgrounds".

Using sounds to customize your iPad

Another great way to customize your iPad so that it stands out is to customize the different sound alerts it makes. There are custom sound clips that can be sued to notify you when there is a new email, when you send mail, text tomes, reminders alerts as well as custom ringtones; custom ringtones are very handy for those who love to use FaceTime. There are different custom sounds that include a bell, a telegraph, a train, a horn or even sounds of magic spells being cast.

New mail and sent mail

The truth of the matter is that ringtones are not only meant for phones, you can use FaceTime to place and receive calls using your iPad. If you plan to use the video conferencing software, why not create a good sound to go with it.

Changing your iPad's ringtone is not a herculean task, there are custom texts you can choose from; this is the sound that the iPad plays whenever a new text message is received.

Select your iPad's "Settings" icon and select "Sounds" on the left hand side menu under the window "general. Select "Text Tone" or "Ringtone" when the sounds menu pops up. The page that follows will have a list of all the custom sounds that are available for use as text tomes or ringtones. You can get a preview of any sound you are interested in choosing by tapping on it. Once you have selected, all you need to do is to exit the Settings App.

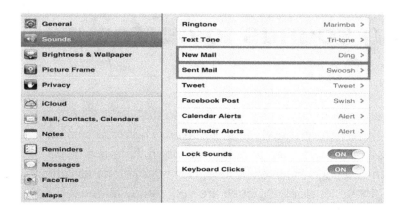

Facebook and Twitter post iPad sounds

Take note that you are not tied down with the default tweet sounds your iPad produces; take just a few minutes to customize your iPad sounds so you can change the sound when you are posting on Facebook or getting a twitter update. Do you want to your Facebook post to sound like a car horn or your Tweeter updates to sound like a spell is being cast on a Disney movie? No problem, simply follow these simple instructions.

After you open your iPad's "Settings", select sounds on the left hand side menu. Choose "Facebook Post" or "Tweet" when the menu pops up. You will see a new list having alert sounds that are available as well as the standard ringtones below each alert. Choose your favorite sound and tap the "Sound" button on top of the screen so you can customize the new sound; exit after you are done.

General	Ringtone	Marimba >
Sounds	Text Tone	Tri-tone >
Brightness & Wallpaper	New Mail	Ding >
Picture Frame	Sent Mail	Swoosh >
Privacy	Tweet	Tweet >
iCloud	Facebook Post	Swish >
Mail, Contacts, Calendars	Calendar Alerts	Alert >
Notes	Reminder Alerts	Alert >
Reminders	Lock Sounds	ON
Messages	Keyboard Clicks	ON
FaceTime		

Calendar and reminder alert sounds

You probably have set reminders on your iPad but you can't stand the default sound on your iPad; nothing to worry about. Customizing the calendar and reminder sounds on your device should not be difficult. You may want to change the calendar event sound to chime or the reminder to sound like a News flash following these simple directions:

Start by going to the iPad's Settings and on the left hand side menu select "Sounds". Choose "Reminder Alerts" of "Calendar Alerts" on the sounds list. The screen that pops up contains a long list of sounds and alerts; you will find standard ringtones listed beneath those clips in case you don't like the alerts. Select you favorite sound and exit or simply tap on the "Sounds" button at the top to customize the ringtone or mail sound.

Turning off keyboard clicks on your iPad

There are those among us who get annoyed by those clicking sounds the iPad keyboard makes; perhaps you are watching a movie and you want to quiet down. While the clicking is helpful whenever you want to be sure you touched a key especially when you are typing in a hurry, this sounds can irritate at times and you may want the entire thing to go silent. The good news is that your iPad's keyboard clicks can be turned off easily.

38

Open your iPads "Settings" and on the left hand side menu select "Sounds". Just slide the On/Off button that is next to "keyboard Clicks" to make sure it is in the "Off" position.

Remember that you can also turn off the sound made by your iPad every time you unlock it on or perhaps customize it to a different sound such as a ringtone of any kind.

Secure your iPad and lock it up

The one very important thing you cannot afford to forget is the security of your device. You should know that you can actually lock up your iPad using an alphanumeric password or a 4-digit passcode. You can also turn on several restrictions that will disable some functions or select Apps. You may even want to restrict the Apps Store so your kids cannot download Apps you don't approve of as well as turning You Tube completely off.

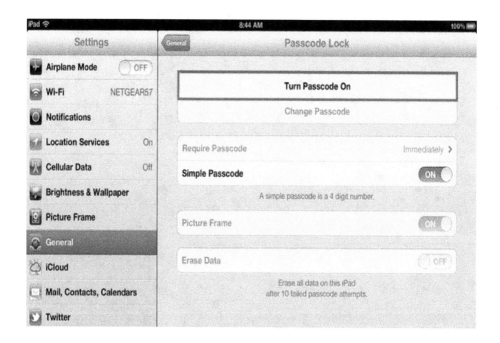

Using a Password of Passcode to protect your iPad

Unknown to many iPad owners, this device is actually a miniature PC and, as such, it can be sued to access loads of information together with what you may not approve that everyone else gets to see. There are a number of good reasons why anyone will want to keep their iPad secure and locked.

You may have young children in your household and you want to make sure they don't use your iPad to get unrestricted access to the internet. Creating a passcode on your iPad will keep it off limits for these young and curious minds. On the other hand, it could be friends who are visiting and who are known to be mischievous or perhaps that co-worker you don't want to automatically log into your Facebook App: simply lock your iPad and you are sure to be safe. You should also know that using a passcode will prevent every Tom, Dick and Harry from snooping around your device should you misplace it or even lose it.

The good news is that locking your iPad is a walk in the park and that simple action keeps it secure from any unrestricted access. You have a choice o fusing a 4-digit passcode like your ATM card or perhaps an alphanumeric password.

You start the short process by going to your iPad's settings and on the left hand side menu locate "General Settings". When you touch "General" the settings will be loaded into the right hand side window.

Select the "Select Passcode Lock" option that you will find below the "Auto-Lock" just below the "Spotlight Search". When you choose this option the iPad will automatically load a screen similar to the one above.

Before locking the iPad you will be required select an alphanumeric password of any length and a 4-digit passcode. Anyone trying to use your iPad who doesn't in put the correct passcode/password and enters a wrong several times will be locked out; the iPad starts with a minute lockout, followed by a five minute lockout before it becomes disabled completely. You can learn how to unlock the iPad after it has been disabled.

Your consideration when selecting the passcode or password should be based on who you are trying to keep away from your iPad. If you are simply trying to restrict children or other family members within the household or perhaps friends visiting, a simple 4-digit passcode should suffice. If you are worried that you could lose your iPad or it could be stolen, you go the extra step and use the longer alphanumeric password for enhanced security. Move the "On" switch you find next to "Simple Passcode" to the "Off" setting to choose an alphanumeric password.

As soon as you touch that button, a window will pop up requesting a password or passcode. You will be requested to enter that passcode or password twice just to be sure you don't enter a wrong passcode accidentally. The iPad will ask for this code every time you want to use it and it is also triggered every time you wake the iPad up before you begin using it. The passcode will be required every time you want to go back to the passcode settings; this prevents you from turning off the iPad are changing the passcode before you enter it.

It is also possible to place restrictions on your iPad such that some features such as You Tube or Safari Browser are turned off. You can also restrict the download of Apps that you feel are inappropriate for particular age groups.

Conclusion

Your iPad is a companion that can help you do so much: from playing games, reading, taking videos and pictures and communicating with the whole world. What about shopping online, keeping your tight schedule and you can be sure the list is endless. While there is no limit to what your iPad can do for you, the few tricks you have learned in this guide should enhance your experience using this wonderful device. Keep on discovering and you will be glad you bought one.

www.ScottsdaleBookPublishing.com

ISBN 9781508423423

9 781508 423423

90000 >